Christmas Oratorio

Bob Chilcott

*for soloists, SATB chorus, and small ensemble
or organ and flute*

vocal score

MUSIC DEPARTMENT

OXFORD
UNIVERSITY PRESS

OXFORD
UNIVERSITY PRESS

Great Clarendon Street, Oxford OX2 6DP,
United Kingdom

Oxford University Press is a department of the University of Oxford.
It furthers the University's objective of excellence in research, scholarship,
and education by publishing worldwide. Oxford is a registered trade mark of
Oxford University Press in the UK and in certain other countries

© Oxford University Press 2019

Bob Chilcott has asserted his right under the Copyright, Designs
and Patents Act, 1988, to be identified as the Composer of this Work

First published 2019

Impression: 4

ISBN 978-0-19-351437-9

Music and text origination by Katie Johnston

Printed in Great Britain on acid-free paper by
Halstan & Co. Ltd, Amersham, Bucks.

Contents

Scoring

The *Christmas Oratorio* is scored for SATB chorus and the following soloists:

Evangelist (tenor)
Gabriel (tenor)
Mary (mezzo-soprano)
Angel (soprano)
Herod (bass)
Simeon (bass)
Mezzo-soprano
Bass

The smaller solo roles (Gabriel, Angel, Herod) may be taken by members of the chorus.

Four of the hymn settings are intended for performance by the audience/congregation in addition to the choir. The melodies are printed with the texts on pp. vi–xii.

Instrumentation

The accompaniment to this work exists in two versions:

1. For small ensemble

flute
2 trumpets in B flat
horn in F
trombone
tuba
timpani
harp
organ (using the part available on hire/rental)

Full scores, vocal scores, and instrumental parts are available on hire/rental from the publisher's Hire Library or appropriate agent.

2. For organ and flute

The organist plays from the vocal score. A separate flute part is printed on pp. 110–115.

Composer's note

This setting of the Christmas story begins with the visitation of the Angel Gabriel to Mary as told in the familiar words of St Luke's Gospel. We hear of the journey of Mary and Joseph to Bethlehem and of the birth of the baby Jesus. After hearing of the birth from an angel, the shepherds come to visit the newborn child. We then hear of the journey of the three wise men, as told in the Gospel of St Matthew, and also how Herod the king tries to win their trust. The piece ends with the presentation of Jesus to the old man Simeon in the temple.

As this work was written for the Three Choirs Festival and was first performed by the three Cathedral Choirs of Gloucester, Worcester, and Hereford in Gloucester Cathedral, it seemed appropriate to include settings of both the Magnificat (Mary's Song) and the Nunc dimittis (The Song of Simeon). These canticles have been sung or spoken every day at the service of Evensong for hundreds of years in cathedrals and churches across the land. They are focal points in the liturgy of this service, as they are also in the story of the birth of Jesus as written in the Gospel of St Luke. I have also included hymn settings, to be sung by both choir and congregation or audience, that punctuate various points in the story, such as the foretelling of the birth of Jesus, the angel appearing to the shepherds, and the journey of the three kings to Bethlehem. The piece, which also includes settings for the choir of well-known Christmas texts by Percy Dearmer, Christina Rossetti, and Robert Herrick, is bookended by two different translations of the fifteenth-century German hymn 'Es ist ein Ros entsprungen'. The medieval image of a rose depicts the prophesy of Isaiah who declared: 'There shall come forth a rod out of the stem of Jesse, and a branch shall grow out of his roots'.

It has been a privilege for me to be able to write a piece involving a story told through biblical texts and verse in English that I know so well through my life as both a singer and composer writing within the tradition of church music here in this country. I am deeply grateful to my dear friend who commissioned the piece; to Adrian Partington and the Three Choirs Festival, who brought the piece to life; and to Griselda Sherlaw-Johnson and my editor, Laura Jones, at Oxford University Press.

Duration: *c.*50 minutes

This note may be reproduced as required for programme notes.

Texts

These texts and melodies may be reproduced as required for programme notes and to allow audience/congregation participation in the hymns during a performance of the *Christmas Oratorio*.

1. Hymn: Lo! how a rose e'er blooming (Choir only)

vv. 1 & 2 16th-cent. German, trans. Theodore Baker (1851–1934); v. 3 19th-cent. German, trans. Harriet R. K. Spaeth (1845–1925)

1. Lo! how a Rose, e'er blooming,
   From tender stem hath sprung,
   Of Jesse's lineage coming
   As seers of old have sung;
   It came, a blossom bright,
   Amid the cold of winter
   When half-spent was the night.

2. Isaiah 'twas foretold it,
   The Rose I have in mind;
   With Mary we behold it,
   The Virgin Mother kind:
   To show God's love aright
   She bore to us a Saviour
   When half-spent was the night.

3. O Flower, whose fragrance tender
   With sweetness fills the air,
   Dispel in glorious splendour
   The darkness everywhere;
   True man, yet very God,
   From sin and death now save us
   And share our every load.

2. The Angel Gabriel

Luke 1: 26–35

And in the sixth month the Angel Gabriel was sent from God unto a city of Galilee, named Nazareth, To a virgin espoused to a man whose name was Joseph, of the house of David; And the virgin's name was Mary. And the angel came in unto her and said, Hail, thou that art highly favoured, The Lord is with thee: blessed art thou among women. And when she saw him, she was troubled at his saying, and cast in her mind what manner of salutation this should be. And the angel said unto her, Fear not, Mary: For thou hast found favour with God. And, behold, thou shalt conceive in thy womb, And bring forth a son, and shalt call his name JESUS. He shall be great, and shall be called the Son of the Highest: and the Lord God shall give unto him the throne of his father David: And he shall reign over the house of Jacob for ever; and of his kingdom there shall be no end. Then said Mary unto the angel, How shall this be, seeing I know not a man? And the angel answered and said unto her, The Holy Ghost shall come upon thee, And the power of the Highest shall overshadow thee: therefore also that holy thing which shall be born of thee shall be called the Son of God.

3. Magnificat

Luke 1: 46–55

My soul doth magnify the Lord: and my spirit hath rejoiced in God my Saviour.
For he hath regarded: the lowliness of his hand-maiden.

Magnificat anima mea Dominum. Et exultavit spiritus meus in Deo salutari meo.
Quia respexit humilitatem ancillae suae:

For behold, from henceforth: all generations shall call me blessed.

For he that is mighty hath magnified me: and holy is his Name.

And his mercy is on them that fear him: throughout all generations.

He hath shewed strength with his arm: he hath scattered the proud in the imagination of their hearts.

He hath put down the mighty from their seat: and hath exalted the humble and meek.

He hath filled the hungry with good things: and the rich he hath sent empty away.

He remembering his mercy hath holpen his servant Israel: as he promised to our forefathers, Abraham, and his seed, for ever.

Glory be to the Father, and to the Son: and to the Holy Ghost; as it was in the beginning, is now, and ever shall be: world without end. Amen.

Ecce enim ex hoc beatam me dicent omnes generationes.

Quia fecit mihi magna qui potens est: et sanctum nomen ejus.

Et misericordia ejus a progenie in progenies; timentibus eum.

Fecit potentiam in brachio suo; dispersit superbos mente cordis sui.

Deposuit potentes de sede; et exaltavit humiles.

Esurientes implevit bonis, et divites dimisit inanes.

Suscepit Israel puerum suum, recordatus misericordiae suae. Sicut locutus est ad patres nostros; Abraham et semini ejus in saecula.

Gloria Patri, et Filio; et Spiritui Sancto. Sicut erat in principio, et nunc, et semper; et in saecula saeculorum. Amen.

4. Hymn: Thou whose almighty word

Music: Bob Chilcott; Words: John Marriott (1780–1825)

BOWEN

(organ)

1. Thou whose almighty word
   Chaos and darkness heard,
   And took their flight;
   Hear us, we humbly pray,
   And where the Gospel-day
   Sheds not its glorious ray
   Let there be light!

2. Thou who didst come to bring
   On thy redeeming wing
   Healing and sight,
   Health to the sick in mind,
   Sight to the inly blind,
   Ah! now to all mankind
   Let there be light!

3. Spirit of truth and love,
   Life-giving, holy Dove,
   Speed forth thy flight!
   Move on the waters' face,
   Bearing the lamp of grace,
   And in earth's darkest place
   Let there be light!

4. Blessed and holy Three,
   Glorious Trinity,
   Wisdom, Love, Might;
   Boundless as ocean's tide
   Rolling in fullest pride,
   Through the world far and wide
   Let there be light!

5. And it came to pass

Luke 2: 1–7

And it came to pass in those days, that there went out a decree from Caesar Augustus that all the world should be taxed. And all went to be taxed, every one into his own city. And Joseph also went up from Galilee, out of the city of Nazareth, into Judaea, unto the city of David, which is called Bethlehem; To be taxed with Mary, his espoused wife, being great with child. And so it was, that, while they were there, the days were accomplished that she should be delivered. And she brought forth her firstborn son, and wrapped him in swaddling clothes, and laid him in a manger; because there was no room for them in the inn.

6. A Boy was born

German chorale 'Ein Kind geborn zu Bethlehem', trans. Percy Dearmer (1867–1936)

A Boy was born in Bethlehem;
Rejoice for that, Jerusalem!
Alleluia.

He let himself a servant be,
That all mankind he might set free:
Alleluia.

Then praise the Word of God who came
To dwell within a human frame:
Alleluia.

7. And there were in the same country shepherds

Luke 2: 8–15

And there were in the same country shepherds abiding in the field, keeping watch over their flock by night. And, lo, the angel of the Lord came upon them, and the glory of the Lord shone round about them: and they were sore afraid. And the angel said unto them, Fear not: for, behold, I bring you good tidings of great joy, which shall be to all people. For unto you is born this day in the city of David a Saviour, which is Christ the Lord. And this shall be a sign unto you; Ye shall find the babe wrapped in swaddling clothes, lying in a manger. And suddenly there was with the angel a multitude of the heavenly host praising God and saying, Glory to God in the highest, and on earth peace, good will toward men. And it came to pass, as the angels were going away from them into heaven, the shepherds said one to another, Let us now go even unto Bethlehem, and see this thing which is come to pass, which the Lord hath made known unto us.

8. Hymn: Shepherds, in the field abiding

Music: Bob Chilcott; Words: George Ratcliffe Woodward (1848–1934)

LAURA

(organ)

1. Shepherds, in the field abiding,
   Tell us, when the seraph bright
   Greeted you with wondrous tiding,
   What you saw and heard that night.
   Gloria, gloria in excelsis Deo. [repeat]

2. We beheld (it is no fable)
   God incarnate, King of bliss,
   Swathed and cradled in a stable,
   And the angel strain was this:
   Gloria, gloria in excelsis Deo. [repeat]

3. Choristers on high were singing
   Jesus and his virgin-birth;
   Heav'nly bells the while a-ringing
   'Peace, goodwill to men on earth.'
   Gloria, gloria in excelsis Deo. [repeat]

4. Thanks, good herdmen, true your story;
   Have with you to Bethlehem:
   Angels hymn the King of Glory;
   Carol we with you and them.
   Gloria, gloria in excelsis Deo. [repeat]

9. And they came with haste

Luke 2: 16–19

And they came with haste, and found Mary, Joseph, and the babe lying in a manger. And when they had seen it, they made known abroad the saying which was told them concerning this child. And all they that heard it wondered at those things which were told them by the shepherds. But Mary kept all these things, and pondered them in her heart.

10. Love came down at Christmas

Christina Rossetti (1830–94)

Love came down at Christmas,
Love all lovely, Love divine;
Love was born at Christmas,
Star and angels gave the sign.

Worship we the Godhead,
Love incarnate, Love divine;
Worship we our Jesus:
But wherewith for sacred sign?

Love shall be our token,
Love be yours and love be mine,
Love to God and all men,
Love for plea and gift and sign.

11. Now when Jesus was born in Bethlehem

Matthew 2: 1–11

Now when Jesus was born in Bethlehem of Judaea in the days of Herod the king, behold, there came wise men from the east to Jerusalem, Saying, Where is he that is born King of the Jews? for we have seen his star in the east, and are come to worship him. When Herod the king had heard these things he was troubled, and all Jerusalem with him. And when he had gathered all the chief priests and scribes of the people together, he demanded of them where Christ should be born. And they said unto him, In Bethlehem of Judaea: for thus it is written by the prophet, And thou Bethlehem, in the land of Juda, art not the least among the princes of Juda: for out of thee shall come a Governor, that shall rule my people Israel. Then Herod, when he had privily called the wise men, enquired of them diligently what time the star appeared. And he sent them to Bethlehem, and said, Go and search diligently for the young child; and when ye have found him, bring me word again, that I may come and worship him also. When they had heard the king, they departed; and, lo, the star, which they saw in the east, went before them, till it came and stood over where the young child was. When they saw the star, they rejoiced with exceeding great joy. And when they were come into the house, they saw the young child with Mary his mother, and fell down, and worshipped him; and when they had opened their treasures, they presented unto him gifts; gold, and frankincense, and myrrh.

12. A Carol to the King

Robert Herrick (1591–1674)

Tell us, thou clear and heavenly tongue,
Where is the babe but lately sprung?
Lies he the lily-banks among?

Or say, if this new birth of ours
Sleeps, laid within some ark of flowers,
Spangled with dew-light; thou canst clear
All doubts, and manifest the where.

Declare to us, bright star, if we shall seek
Him in the morning's blushing cheek,
Or search the beds of spices through,
To find him out?

(*Star:*) No, this ye need not do;
But only come, and see him rest,
A princely babe, in's mother's breast.

13. Hymn: As with gladness men of old

Music: Bob Chilcott; Words: William Chatterton Dix (1837–98)

PATERSON

1. As with gladness men of old
   Did the guiding star behold,
   As with joy they hailed its light,
   Leading onward, beaming bright,
   So, most gracious God, may we
   Evermore be led to thee. [*repeat*]

2. As with joyful steps they sped
   To that lowly manger-bed,
   There to bend the knee before
   Him whom heav'n and earth adore,
   So may we with willing feet
   Ever seek thy mercy-seat. [*repeat*]

3. As they offered gifts most rare
   At that manger rude and bare,
   So may we with holy joy,
   Pure, and free from sin's alloy,
   All our costliest treasures bring,
   Christ, to thee our heav'nly King. [*repeat*]

4. Holy Jesu, every day
   Keep us in the narrow way;
   And, when earthly things are past,
   Bring our ransomed souls at last
   Where they need no star to guide,
   Where no clouds thy glory hide. [*repeat*]

5. In the heav'nly country bright
   Need they no created light;
   Thou its light, its joy, its crown,
   Thou its sun which goes not down:
   There for ever may we sing
   Alleluias to our King. [*repeat*]

14. And when eight days were accomplished

Luke 2: 21, 25–8

And when eight days were accomplished, his name was called JESUS, which was so named of the angel before he was conceived in the womb. And, behold, there was a man in Jerusalem, whose name was Simeon; and the same man was just and devout, waiting for the consolation of Israel: and the Holy Ghost was upon him. And it was revealed unto him by the Holy Ghost, that he should not see death, before he had seen the Lord's Christ. And he came by the Spirit into the temple; and when the parents brought in the child Jesus, to do for him after the custom of the law, Then took he him up in his arms, and blessed God, and said,

15. Nunc dimittis

Luke 2: 29–32

Lord, now lettest thou thy servant depart in peace, according to thy word; For mine eyes have seen thy salvation, Which thou hast prepared before the face of all people; A light to lighten the Gentiles, and the glory of thy people Israel.

Glory be to the Father, and to the Son: and to the Holy Ghost; as it was in the beginning, is now, and ever shall be: world without end. Amen.

16. And Joseph and his mother marvelled at those things

Luke 2: 33–4, 39

And Joseph and his mother marvelled at those things which were spoken of him. And Simeon blessed them, and said unto Mary his mother, Behold, this child is set for the fall and rising again of many in Israel. And when they had performed all things according unto the law of the Lord, they returned into Galilee, to their own city Nazareth.

17. Hymn: A great and mighty wonder

Music: Bob Chilcott; Words: St Germanus (634–c.734), trans. J. M. Neale (1818–66)

PARTINGTON

* On the second repeat, there are only three ♩ rests before verse 3 begins.

1. A great and mighty wonder,
    A full and holy cure!
    The Virgin bears the Infant
    With virgin-honour pure.
    Repeat, repeat the hymn again, the hymn again:
    'To God on high be glory,
    And peace on earth to men!'

2. The Word becomes incarnate
    And yet remains on high!
    And cherubim sing anthems
    To shepherds from the sky.
    Repeat, repeat the hymn again, the hymn again:
    'To God on high be glory,
    And peace on earth to men!'

3. Since all he comes to ransom,
    By all he is adored,
    The Infant born in Bethlehem,
    The Saviour and the Lord.
    Repeat, repeat the hymn again, the hymn again:
    'To God on high be glory,
    And peace on earth to men!'

Christmas Oratorio

Commissioned by the Three Choirs Festival with the generous support of an anonymous donor

CHRISTMAS ORATORIO

PART 1

1. Hymn: Lo! how a Rose e'er blooming

16th-cent. (vv. 1 & 2) and 19th-cent. (v. 3) German
vv. 1 & 2 trans. Theodore Baker (1851–1934);
v. 3 trans. Harriet R. K. Spaeth (1845–1925)

BOB CHILCOTT

'PARTINGTON'

Printed in Great Britain

OXFORD UNIVERSITY PRESS, MUSIC DEPARTMENT, GREAT CLARENDON STREET, OXFORD OX2 6DP

3

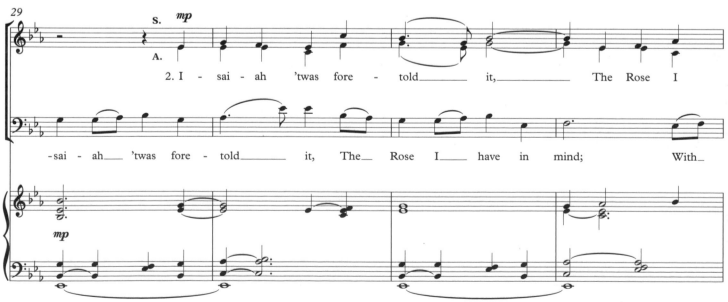

When half-spent was the night.

DESCANT SOPRANOS

unis.

ALL OTHER VOICES *f*

3. O

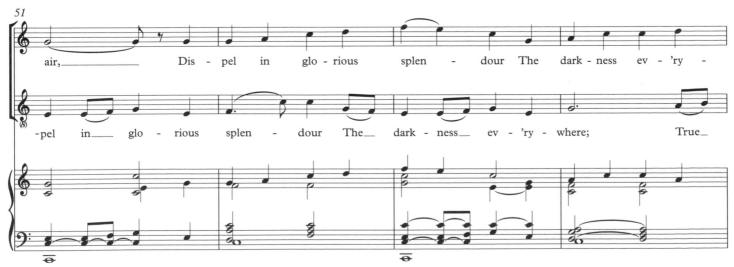

(DESCANT SOPRANOS) *f*

3. O Flower, whose fra-grance ten - der With sweet-ness fills the

Flower, whose fra-grance ten - der With sweet-ness fills the air, Dis -

air, Dis-pel in glo-rious splen - dour The dark-ness ev-'ry-

-pel in glo-rious splen - dour The dark-ness ev-'ry-where; True

2. *The Angel Gabriel*

Luke 1: 26–35

GABRIEL (TENOR)

Hail, hail,— thou that art high - ly fa - voured, The

Lord is with thee: blessed art thou a - mong— wo - men.—

EVANGELIST

And when she saw him,— she was troub-led at his say - ing,

67

And, be-hold, thou shalt con-ceive in thy womb, And bring forth a

Man.

71

son, and shalt call his name JE -

Ped.

75

-SUS. He shall be great, and shall be

Man.

king - dom there shall— be no end.

EVANGELIST
Then said— Ma - ry un - to the— an - gel,—

Man.

slightly slower

MARY
How shall this be, see - ing I know not a man?—

106 a tempo

EVANGELIST
mp
And the an - gel an - swered and said un - to her,

a tempo
mp

111 broader
mf

GABRIEL
mf
The Ho - ly Ghost shall come up - on thee, And the

broader
mf
Ped.

115
power of the High - est shall o - ver - sha - dow thee:

3. Magnificat

Luke 1: 46–55

and my spi - rit hath re - joiced in God my

me - us in De - o sa - lu - ta - ri me - o.

unis. **p**

Qui - a

M-S SOLO **mp**

Sa - viour, my Sa - viour, my

T./B. **mp**

re - spe - xit hu - mi - li - ta - tem an - cil - lae su - ae: Ec - ce e - nim ex

Ped.

Sa - viour.

p

hoc be - a - tam me di - cent om - nes ge - ne - ra - ti - o - nes.

p

Man. Ped.

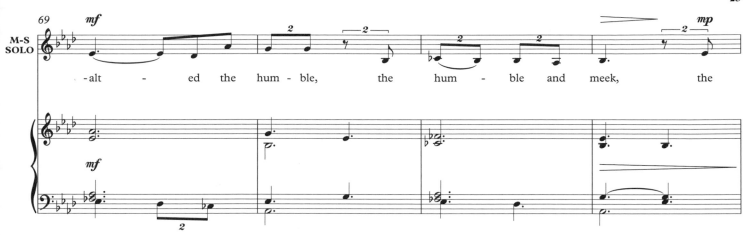

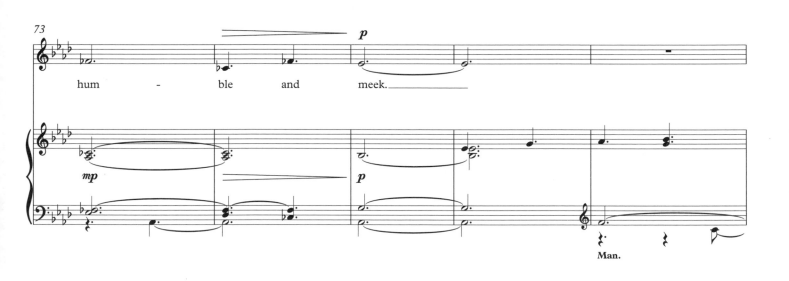

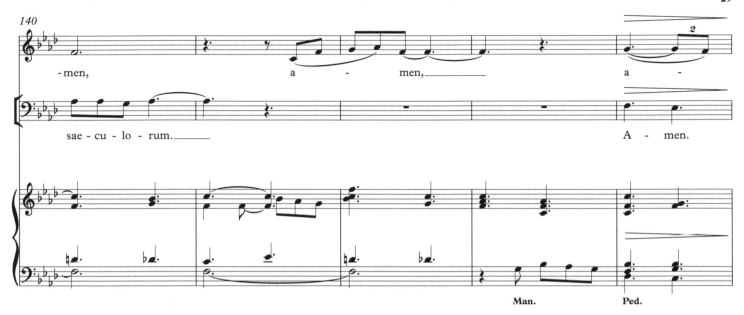

4. Hymn: Thou whose almighty word

John Marriott (1780–1825)

'BOWEN'

5. And it came to pass in those days

Luke 2: 1–7

was, that, while they were there, the days were ac - com - plished that

she should be de - liv - ered.

And she brought forth her first - born son, and

wrapped_____ him in_____ swad - dling clothes,_____ and

laid him_____ in_____ a man - - ger;_____

Man.

rit.

be - cause there was no_____ room for_____

Ped.

slower

them in the_____ inn.

6. A Boy was born

German chorale 'Ein Kind geborn zu Bethlehem'
trans. Percy Dearmer (1867–1936)

PART 2

7. And there were in the same country shepherds

Luke 2: 8–15

be to all____ peo - ple.

for,_ be - hold, I bring_ you good tid - ings of great____ joy, which shall

For un - to you is born this day in the ci - ty of Da - vid a

Man.

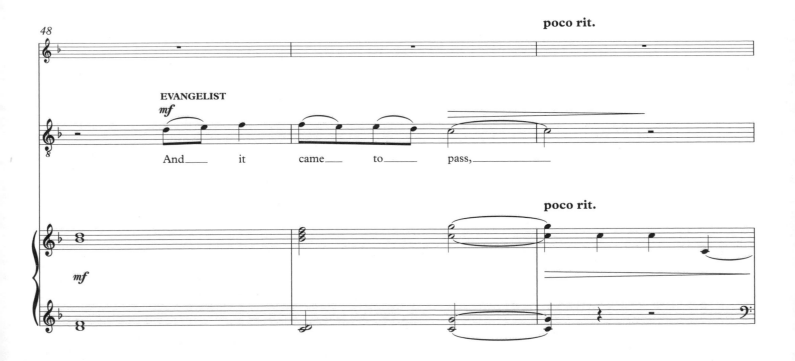

8. Hymn: Shepherds, in the field abiding

George Ratcliffe Woodward (1848–1934)

'LAURA'

9. And they came with haste

Luke 2: 16–19

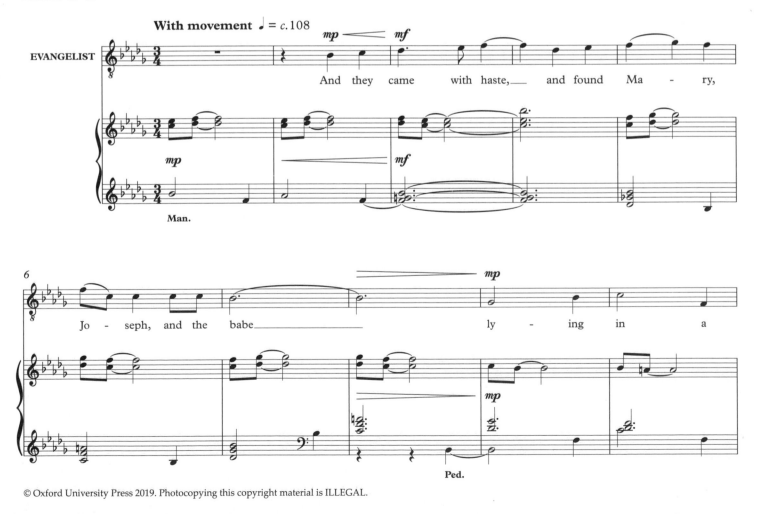

30 won-dered at those things,_____ those___ things which were

35 told them by___ the shep - herds._____

a little slower
40 *pp legato espress.*
But Ma - ry kept all these things, and pon - dered

pp legato espress.

Ped.

45 **rit.**
them in___ her heart.___

10. Love came down at Christmas

Christina Rossetti (1830–94)

PART 3

11. *Now when Jesus was born in Bethlehem*

Matthew 2: 1–11

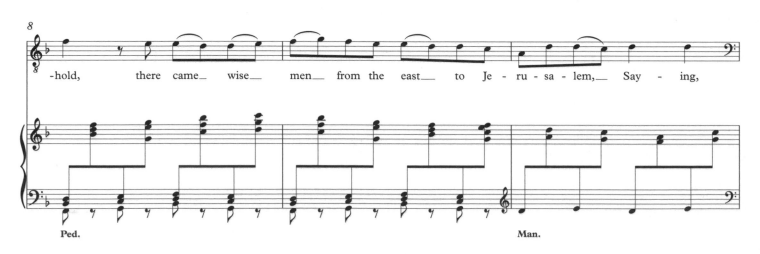

WISE MEN (CHORUS)

Where is he____ that is born King of the Jews? for we have seen his star____ in the east, and are come to wor - ship him.

EVANGELIST

When He - rod the king had____ heard____ these____ things____ he was troub - led, and all Je - ru - sa - lem____ with him.____ And

when he had ga-thered all the chief priests and scribes of the peo - ple to - ge - ther,

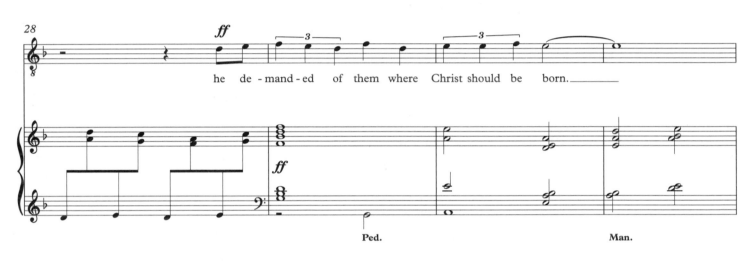

he de - mand - ed of them where Christ should be born.___

(EVANGELIST)

And they said un - to him,

CHIEF PRIESTS (CHORUS)

In

S.
A.

T.
B.

pri - vi - ly__ called__ the wise men, en - quired of them di - li - gent - ly what

time the star__ ap - peared. And he

sent them to Beth - le - hem, and said,_____

Ped.   Man.

HEROD (BASS)

Go and search di - li - gent - ly for the young child;_____ and

Ped.

-part - ed; and, lo, the star, which they saw in the east, went be - fore them,

till it came and stood o - ver where the young child was.

p dolce, flessibile

When they saw the star, they re -

-joiced with ex - ceed - ing great joy. And

p dolce, flessibile

Man.

Ped.

mp

they pre- sent- ed un- to him gifts; gold, and frank- in- cense, and myrrh,_____ gold, and frank- in- cense, and myrrh._____

Man.

rit.

p

Ped.

12. A Carol to the King

Robert Herrick (1591–1674)

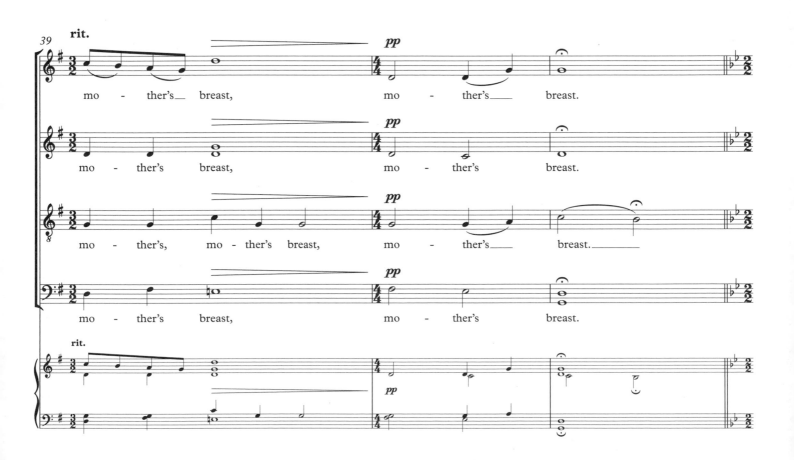

13. Hymn: As with gladness men of old

William Chatterton Dix (1837–98)

'PATERSON'

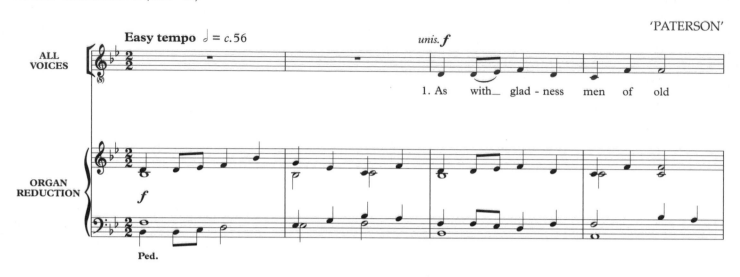

14

led to thee, ev - er - more be led to thee.

S./A. *unis.*

19 *mf*

S./A.

2. As with joy - ful steps they sped To that low - ly man - ger - bed, There to bend the

Man.

24

knee be - fore Him whom heav'n and earth a - dore, So may we with will - ing feet

Ped.

29

Ev - er seek thy mer - cy - seat, ev - er seek thy mer - cy - seat.

PART 4

14. And when eight days were accomplished

Luke 2: 21, 25–8

92

46

- on him.

51 *pp*

And it was re - vealed un - to him by the Ho - ly Ghost, that he should not see

Man.

56

death, be - fore he had seen the

61 **rit.**

Lord's Christ.

15. Nunc dimittis

Luke 2: 29–32

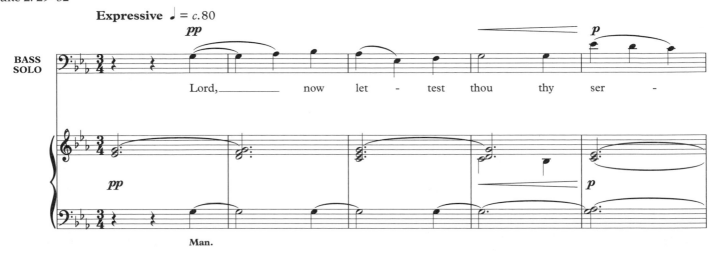

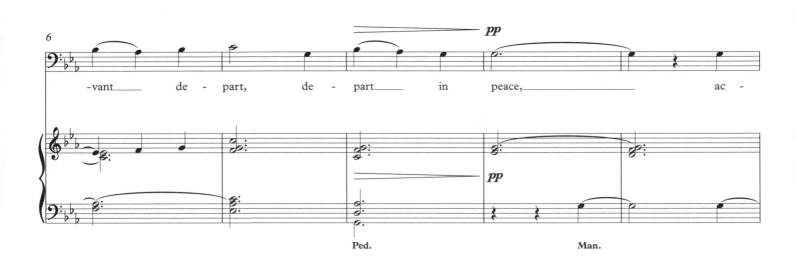

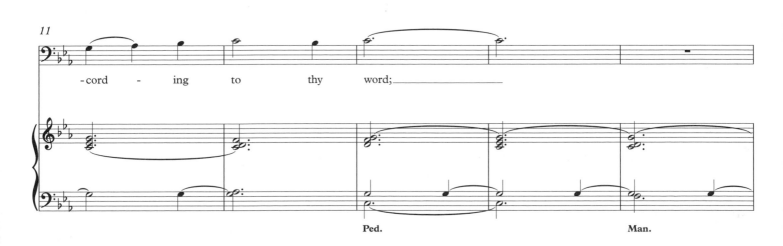

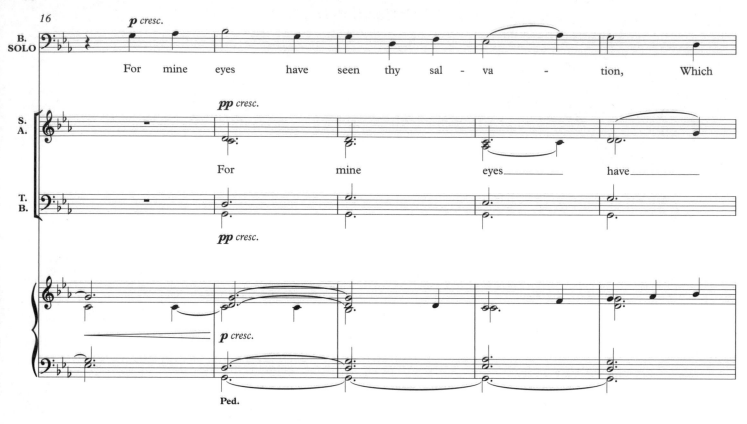

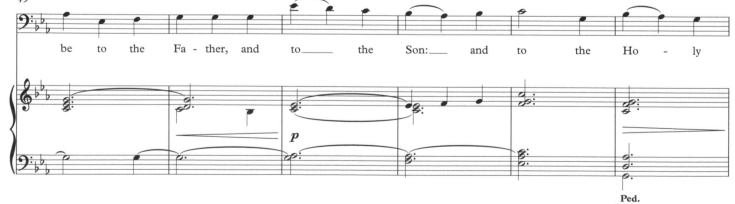

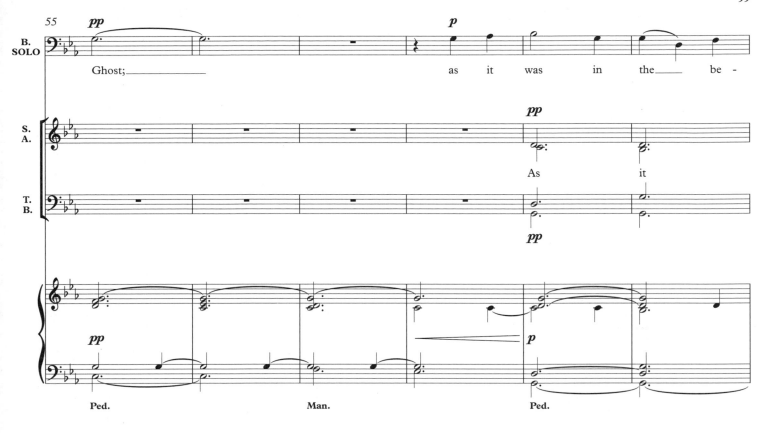

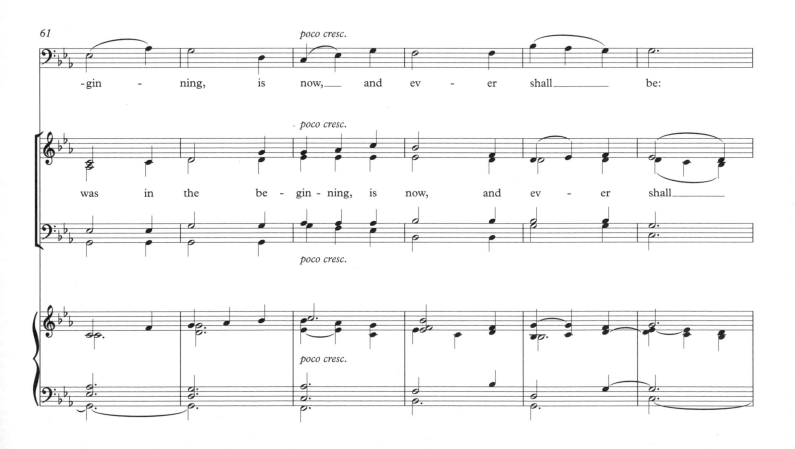

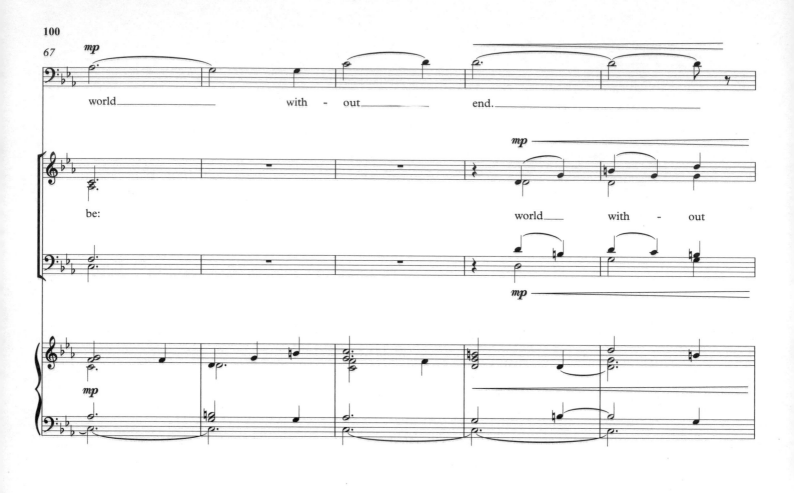

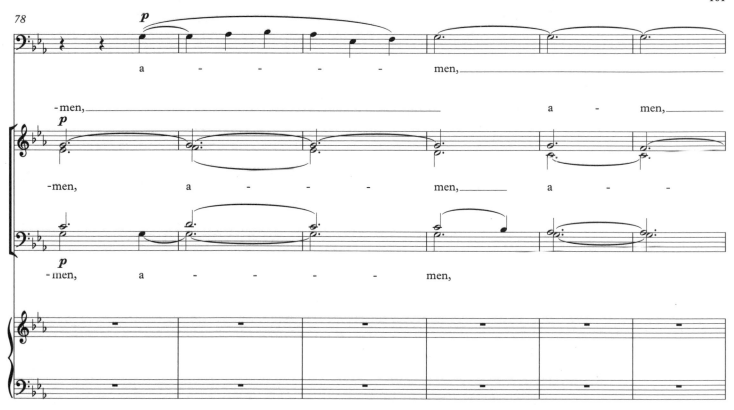

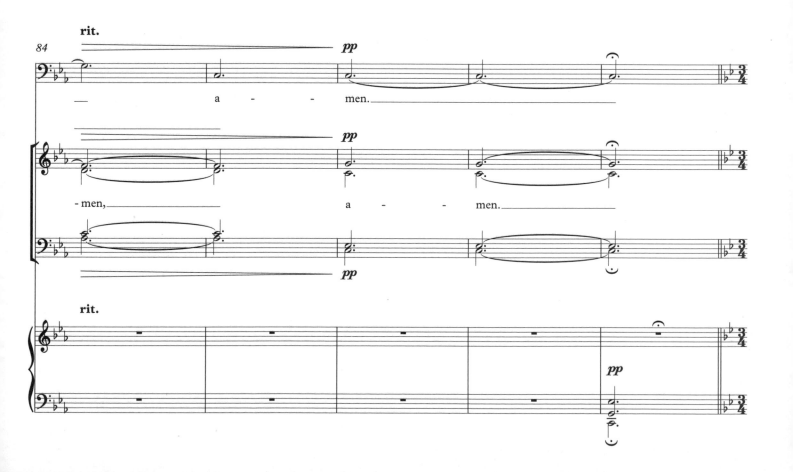

16. And Joseph and his mother marvelled at those things

Luke 2: 33–4, 39

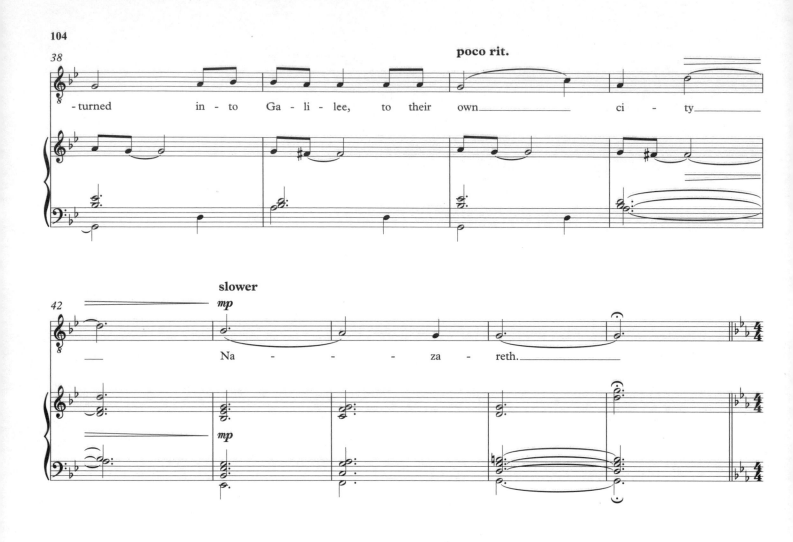

17. Hymn: A great and mighty wonder

St Germanus (634–*c*.734)
trans. J. M. Neale (1818–66)

'PARTINGTON'

-gain: 'To God on high be glo - ry, And peace on

earth to men!'

Man.

Ped.

2. The Word be - comes in -

42

glo - ry, And peace on earth to men!'

unis.

46 **DESCANT SOPRANOS** *f*

3. Since all he comes to ran - som, By

ALL OTHER VOICES *unis. f*

3. Since all he comes to ran - som, By all he is a -

50

all he is a - dored, The In - fant born in Beth - le - hem, The

-dored, The In - fant born in Beth - le - hem, The Sa - viour and the

SOLO FLUTE

PART 1

1. Lo! how a Rose e'er blooming–TACET

2. The Angel Gabriel

BOB CHILCOTT

3. Magnificat–TACET; 4. Thou whose almighty word–TACET;

5. And it came to pass in those days–TACET; 6. A Boy was born–TACET

SOLO FLUTE

PART 2

7. And there were in the same country shepherds

8. *Shepherds, in the field abiding*–TACET; 9. *And they came with haste*–TACET;

10. *Love came down at Christmas*–TACET

SOLO FLUTE

PART 3—TACET

(11. Now when Jesus was born in Bethlehem; 12. A Carol to the King;
13. As with gladness men of old)

PART 4

14. And when eight days were accomplished